Cambridge Cats

CAMBRIDGE CATS

Tony Jedrej

with text by John Gaskell

Foreword by Mary Archer

Duckworth

First published in 1994 by
Gerald Duckworth & Co. Ltd.
The Old Piano Factory
48 Hoxton Square, London N1
Tel: 071 729 5986
Fax: 071 729 0015

A catalogue record for this book is available from the British Library

ISBN 0 7156 2636 1

Frontispiece: Porter meets college cat in Trinity cloisters

Photoset in North Wales by
Derek Doyle & Associates, Mold, Clwyd
Printed in Great Britain by
Ebenezer Baylis & Son Ltd, Worcester

Contents

Foreword by Mary Archer

I currently have three cats, the latest in a long line of equally loved mongrels and pedigrees – slim twin Abyssinians, one grey and the other red, and a tubby silver tabby. I also have two sons and a husband, of roughly corresponding contours. Whenever I come home – with a sigh of relief – to Grantchester, I can be sure of finding at least one welcoming cat on the mat, although I cannot be sure of finding my husband or either of my sons. Home without my sons is perhaps inevitable, given that they are both in their twenties and at university; home without my frenetically busy husband has become habitual for part of many weeks. But home without the cats would simply not be home.

No animal so dimly acquiescent, so unconditionally slavish as a dog could feel at home in the academic courts of Cambridge, but cats – watchful, self-contained, inscrutable cats – are their natural companions. I venture to think that is how the porters and masters of the colleges whose cats are portrayed in Tony Jedrej's affectionate photographs must view their feline cohabitants.

But judge for yourself how well the cat belongs in the cloister. Look through these photographs, and enjoy the Master's moggy and the Porter's lodger.

The Old Vicarage
Grantchester
14 June 1994

Caiaphas of St John's

Named after the High Priest before whom Christ was tried, Caiaphas exemplifies the status enjoyed by college cats. His nickname is Bush, after his owner, the Chaplain of St John's. Something of a nomad, he has ventured as far north as Churchill College. After a week of sleuthing by a St John's tracker he was detected and collected – a bit of a bruiser with a record of scratching tourists' trusting hands.

Caiaphas of St John's

Caiaphas of St John's

Sam of New Hall

The porters dote on him, yet though he is spoiled with titbits Sam's hunting instincts remain, like his claws, razor-sharp. Japanese visitors to the college, admiring the former gardens of Charles Darwin, were horrified when Sam launched an assault on a squirrel's nest, consuming the entire contents and reducing the guests to tears. A cat to have on your side.

Sam of New Hall

Sam of New Hall

Sam of New Hall

Rose Garrard's fresco panel, *Madonna Cascade*, was donated to New Hall by the artist in 1992 and still intrigues the college cat.

Sam of New Hall

Diddling of Girton

The British Embassy in Luxembourg was once the haunt of Diddling, pictured here with Professor Alec Campbell, whose wife Juliet was British Ambassador there before becoming Mistress of Girton. The Campbells' home is in Oxford, so Diddling commutes between the two universities. 'You'll find her here, there or in a cat basket in between,' says her mistress.

Diddling of Girton

Diddling of Girton

Mum Cat of Robinson

Gollum-like in her feral existence, Mum Cat is rarely visible beyond a pair of eyes gleaming in the undergrowth. But Robinson is the newest Cambridge college and behaviour too *outré* would be unbecoming. A don is entrusted to make up any gaps in her diet not filled by mice, shrews, and so on.

Mum Cat of Robinson

Lucy of Wolfson

Lucy haughtily took possession of Wolfson College two years ago when she came to track down her owner, Derek Cowling, a porter on residential Christmas duty at the time. The Little Madam attitude persists. She would only have her photograph taken, we were told, if she could specify the date and time of her appearance.

Lucy of Wolfson

Lucy poses in the Betty Wu Lee gardens.

Lucy of Wolfson

Lucy of Wolfson

Sox of Pembroke

Sister of the more illustrious Thomasina (see pp. 72-5) Sox is more at home in Pembroke's potting sheds, greenhouses and gardens than in its offices. When their paths do cross, sibling rivalry, including hissing and spitting, immediately breaks out. Sox is fed, groomed and analysed by head gardener Nick Firman who recommends: 'If you've got to come back, come back as a college cat.'

Sox of Pembroke

Sox of Pembroke

Olga of King's

Olga, pictured here with Dusha Bateson, wife of the Provost of King's, is a Russian Blue whose deportment belies her fourteen years. As she grows old gracefully, at least two of her beautiful progeny can be found depicted in oils in New York.

Olga of King's

Olga of King's

Benson of Jesus

Note the proprietorial mien. Benson is perhaps the only Cambridge cat who can claim a democratic right to occupy his premises, having been voted in by the Junior Common Room following his predecessor's death in 1989. Fond of wandering off, he was once returned to the college at 2 a.m. by a concerned resident north of the river. He has good enough reason to return, enjoying honorary dining rights at the college. Not bad for a cat who started life in a home.

Benson of Jesus

Benson of Jesus

Benson of Jesus

Rama and Sita of Selwyn

Rama, the seventh incarnation of Vishnu, has now come back as a cat at Selwyn College with his beautiful companion Sita, their earthly guardians being the new Master, Dr David Harrison and his wife Sheila.

Rama and Sita of Selwyn

Abbey of Ridley Hall

The Anglican postgraduate college of Ridley Hall houses the aptly named Abbey, owned by the Principal, the Rev. Graham Cray. Although her favourite activity is watching college croquet matches, the six-year-old tabby is still able to make a quick exit if necessary (see p. 96).

Abbey of Ridley Hall

Abbey of Ridley Hall

Abbey of Ridley Hall

Thomas of King's

At twenty-two Thomas is one of the oldest cats in Cambridge, his great age attributable perhaps to his enthusiasm for work – he can still keep the vermin down despite his years. His outdoor life is spent in the fresh air at King's College sports ground where he's currently training a sprightly youngster in the finer points of pouncing.

Thomas of King's

Titan of Trinity

Trinity Great Court was the site of the great Caucus Race, immortalised in *Chariots of Fire*, in which athletes had to run almost 400 yards round the court while the Trinity clock struck 12 noon. Today it is viewed with nonchalance by Titan, who arrived at the college with Dr Hugh Hunt but decided to stay when Dr Hunt moved on. Who feeds him now? Ask anyone and the answer will be: 'Everybody!'

Titan of Trinity

Titan of Trinity

Titan of Trinity

Titan of Trinity

Titan of Trinity

Daisy of St Catharine's

Sir Terence English, pioneer heart surgeon and Master of St Catharine's, is not a man usually found on his knees unless he's luring Daisy out for lunch. The cat of St Cat's is of a slightly nervous disposition but Sir Terence's steady hands, holding bowls of milk and Munchies, ensure that the operation is a complete success.

Daisy of St Catharine's

Daisy of St Catharine's

Lloyd of Wesley House

Originally from Norfolk, Lloyd lives a quiet contented life in the Porter's Lodge at Wesley House, the Methodist postgraduate college in Jesus Lane, where his owner Ray James finds him a most unremarkable cat. This, among a collection of eccentrics, is a fame of its own.

Lloyd of Wesley House

Sprocket of Fitzwilliam

Rarely can one cat have been the focus of so much affection. Sprocket is known to all the students and staff at Fitzwilliam where the bar steward keeps a glass jar for contributions to vet's bills. Those so favoured are proud to hang a sign outside their room declaring 'Sprocket slept here,' the feline equivalent of a blue plaque. 'They should commission a statue for this one,' says building superintendent David Holton, a devotee whose Christmas Day includes a journey to college to prepare Sprocket's festive lunch.

Sprocket of Fitzwilliam

Sprocket of Fitzwilliam

Sprocket of Fitzwilliam

Thomasina of Pembroke

Thomasina is the quintessential academic cat, named after Thomas Gray, the Pembroke College poet and author of *Ode on a Favourite Cat, Drowned in a Tub of Goldfish*. Sir Thomas Adams, Professor of Arabic, dedicated his translation of Aristotle's *Rhetoric* to her. One of the fellows explains: 'As befits an academic cat, she uses her intelligence to solve the problem in hand, which usually involves getting food.'

Thomasina of Pembroke

Thomasina of Pembroke

Pusskins of Christ's

The name itself is redolent of pathos and her look says it all: 'You think *you've* had it tough?' Certainly 'Lucky' would be an inappropriate name for a stray with a lame front leg whose home is a car park. But Pusskins survives, lovingly tended and fed twice daily by the Bursar's secretary at Christ's.

Buster of Sidney Sussex

His c.v. the envy of any high-flyer, the universities of Yale, Oxford and now Cambridge have been graced by Buster's handsome features. Today, safely out of quarantine, he is in residence at Sidney Sussex where his peripatetic owner, Dr Claire Preston, is a Fellow. 'But he still can't read or write,' observes one don.

Buster of Sidney Sussex

Buster of Sidney Sussex

Oliver and Peggotty of Wesley House

Oliver and Peggotty, brother and sister, belong to the Principal of Wesley House, Dr Ivor Jones (pictured with Peggotty on p. 85). They are difficult to photograph together, as demonstrated when they were taken to a local photographic studio and left the place looking like a war zone.

Oliver and Peggotty of Wesley House

Peggotty of Wesley House

Bossuet of Gonville and Caius

The 17th-century French churchman Jacques Bénigne Bossuet preached before Louis XIV, achieving a degree of fame now reflected in the name of a two-year-old ginger cat at Gonville and Caius. Bossuet the cat, however, is much less controversial than Bossuet the fiery orator. He gets on well with staff, students, visitors and, of course, his owner, Professor Peter Bayley.

Bossuet of Gonville and Caius

Stan the Cat

After sixteen years of diligent mousing a cat often feels a nap coming on. Stan the Cat's nearest college is Jesus, but he is owned by a former Mayor of Cambridge, Lavena Hawes. Her son, venturing away from the more arcane academic choice of names, christened this one after Stan Bowles, the QPR footballer.

Stan the Cat

The St Catharine's May Ball cat

This papier-mâché grinning Cheshire cat, made for a May Ball, has since retired to take up residence in the college bar.

The St Catharine's May Ball cat

Archie and Oscar of Grantchester

Mary Archer, Oscar and Archie stroll in the gardens of the Old Vicarage at Grantchester while Percy, the Archers' third cat, visits the Orchard Tea Rooms.

Archie and Oscar of Grantchester

Pickwick of Downing

Before his death in 1990, Downing's cat achieved notoriety when he tried to take on an alsatian guard dog accompanying Princess Margaret on an official visit. Pickwick's toughness was attributed to his sleeping rough in shop windows close to the University Arms hotel, his favourite dining spot. He would use the Porters' Lodge letter-box as a cat-flap when he opted to stay in college.

Sam of Jesus

Sam was introduced to college life when he was brought in by a bedmaker. He arrived as a mere waif but rose rapidly in stature and prestige to end his days in the comfort of the Porters' Lodge.

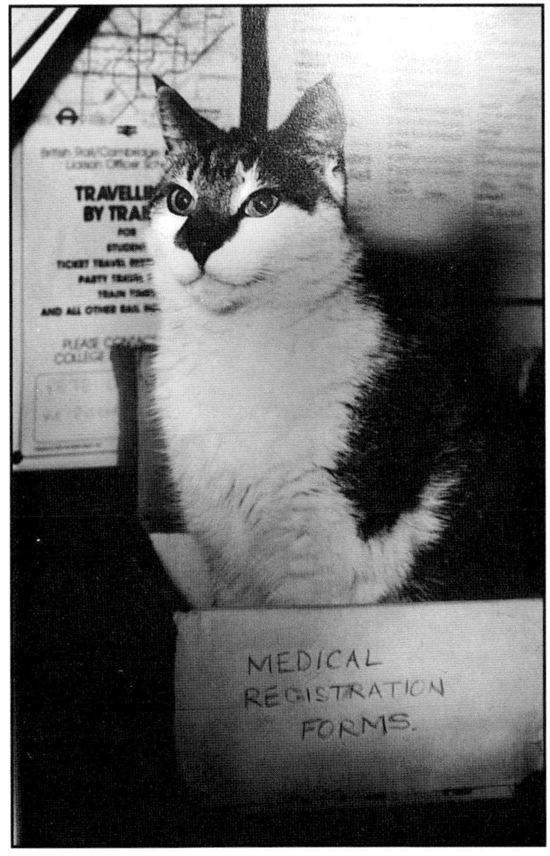

Pickwick of Downing and Sam of Jesus